Table of Contents

Splash!

Pacific chorus frog

Q What happened to the frog's car when it broke down?

A It got toad.

Frogs

Elizabeth Carney

NATIONAL
GEOGRAPHIC

Washington, D.C.

For my parents, Marty and Cindy Carney, who charitably
endured my collections of slimy creatures. — E. C.

Copyright © 2009 National Geographic Society.
This British English edition published in 2017
by Collins, an imprint of HarperCollins*Publishers*,
The News Building, 1 London Bridge Street, London. SE1 9GF.

> Browse the complete Collins catalogue at
> www.collins.co.uk

A catalogue record for this publication is available from the British Library.

ISBN: 978-0-00-826667-7
US Edition ISBN: 978-1-4263-1573-2

Photo credits:
Front Cover: © Digital Vision; 1, 14 (bottom), 27 (top): © Shutterstock; 2: © Michael and Patricia Fogden/CORBIS;
4-5: © Michael Durham/Minden Pictures/Getty Images; 6 (left): © Roger Wilmshurst/Frank Lane Picture Agency/CORBIS;
6 (right): © Pete Oxford/Minden Pictures/Getty Images; 7 (left): © Joe McDonald/CORBIS; 7 (right), 32 (bottom, left):
© Gallo Images/CORBIS; 8, 32 (top, left): © Norbert Wu/Science Faction/Getty Images; 9: © Gerald Lopez/Associated Press; 10,
17: © Mark Moffett/Minden Pictures/Getty Images; 12: © Visuals Unlimited/CORBIS; 13 (top), 21 (top): © Pete Oxford/
Nature Picture Library; 13 (bottom): © Photos.com/Jupiter Images; 14-15: © Buddy Mays/CORBIS; 16: © Steve Winter/National
Geographic/Getty Images; 18 (top), 26 (bottom), 30 (bottom): © Michael and Patricia Fogden/Minden Pictures/Getty Images;
18 (bottom): © Michael Lustbader/drr.net; 19 (top), 24: © Christian Ziegler/Danita Delimont Agency/drr.net; 19 (bottom): ©
Digital Vision; 20: © Liquidlibrary/Jupiter Images; 21 (bottom): © Wegner/ARCO/Nature Picture Library; 22-23: © Glow Imag-
es/Alamy; 25: © Robert Clay/California Stock Photo/drr.net; 26 (top), 32 (top, right): © Paula Gallon; 27
(bottom): © Carol Wien/Mira; 28: © Don Farrall/Photodisc/Getty Images; 29: Geoff Brightling/Dorling
Kindersley/Getty Images; 30 (top): © Geoff Brightling/Dorling Kindersley/DK Images; 31 (top, both):
© Joel Sartore/drr.net; 31 (bottom): © David A. Northcott/CORBIS; 32 (bottom, right): © Sue Daly/Nature Picture Library.

Printed and bound in China by RR Donnelley APS

Splish, splash.
What is that sound?
What is hopping and
jumping around?
What loves to swim?
What loves to eat insects?
It's a frog!
Can you hop like a frog?

Frogs live all over the world, except in Antarctica. Frogs usually live in wet places. They like rivers, lakes and ponds.

Marsh frog

Andean marsupial frog

Antarctica is the continent at the South Pole.

Ribbit!

Habitat: The natural place where a plant or animal lives.

Red-eyed tree frog

Bullfrog

But some frogs live in trees. Some even live in the desert. Wherever they live, that's their habitat.

Croak!

Look at this frog croaking! Some frogs' throats puff up when they make sounds. Each type of frog makes its own sound.

Lake frog

Coqui frog

Ribbit!

Croak: The deep, hoarse noise that a frog makes.

The coqui frog is named after the "CO-KEE!" sound it makes. This frog is only the size of a ten-pence piece. Even small frogs can make loud noises!

Frogs make different sounds
for different reasons. Sometimes
it's to warn other frogs of
danger. Sometimes it's to call
to frogs nearby.

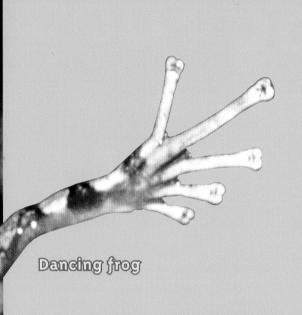

Dancing frog

This frog lives around noisy waterfalls. Other frogs would not be able to hear its calls. So it dances instead! It sticks out one leg, and then the other. Can you dance like this frog?

Frog Food

What is a frog's favourite food? Usually it's insects. Frogs eat dragonflies, crickets and other bugs.

Green frog

Q Why are frogs so happy?

A They eat what bugs them!

Amazon horned frog

Some frogs eat bigger animals like worms and mice. The American bullfrog even eats other frogs!

American bullfrog

13

What's that pink flash? It's how a frog catches insects. It shoots out its long, sticky tongue at a passing insect. The frog pulls the insect into its mouth.

If your tongue were as long as a frog's, it would reach to your belly button!

Green tree frog

Every Size and Colour

Frogs can be many different sizes.

Microfrog

The smallest frog is as big as a fingernail.

The largest is as big as a rabbit.

Goliath frog

Frogs can be different colours, too.

Tiger striped leaf frog

Some are green or brown.

Amazonian poison dart frog

Others have stripes or spots.

Red poison dart frog

Frogs can be red, yellow or orange.

Blue poison dart frog

They can even be bright blue!

Watch Out!

These colourful frogs may look pretty. But watch out! These frogs have poison in their skin. Their bright colour warns enemies not to eat them.

Poison dart frog

Ribbit!

Poison:
Something that can kill or hurt living things.

Poison dart frog

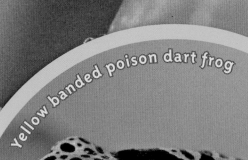

Yellow banded poison dart frog

This little frog is only 2.5 cm long. Its name is Terribilis, which means "the terrible one." How did it get this name? By being the most deadly frog of all! One Terribilis has enough poison to kill 20,000 mice.

Terribilis

Frog Babies

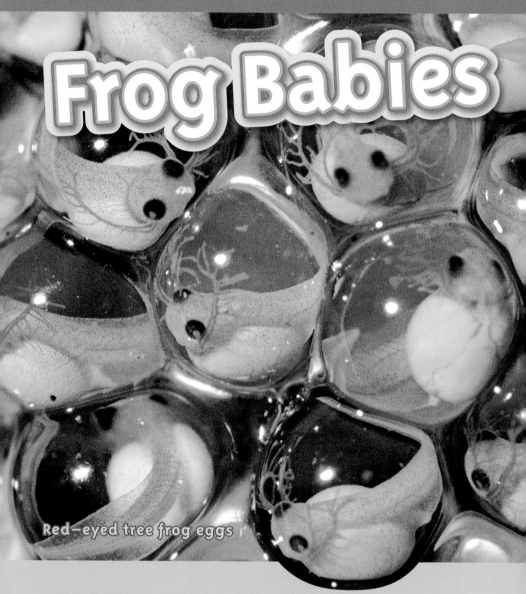

Red—eyed tree frog eggs

All frogs, even the Terribilis, have mothers. Mother frogs lay eggs. When the eggs are ready, out pop the tadpoles!

Tadpoles are baby frogs. But they don't look like frogs yet. Tadpoles have tails. They only live in water.

Pacific tree frog tadpole

Tadpoles grow up to be frogs.

1 At first they breathe underwater with gills.

Gills

Tadpoles

Red-eyed tree frog tadpoles

Ribbit!

Gills: The body parts on the sides of a fish or tadpole through which it breathes.

2 They grow lungs for breathing air.

3 They grow legs for hopping and swimming.

Monkey frog tadpole

4 In three months, they lose their tails.

Bullfrog

It's time to hop out of the water!

Toads Are Frogs, Too!

What's the difference between toads and frogs?

Some frogs are poisonous.

Moist and smooth.

Teeth in upper jaw.

Long, powerful jumping legs; most frogs have webbed back feet.

Eggs laid in clusters or groups.

Toads are a type of frog. Frogs spend most of their lives around water. Toads spend more time on dry land. Their bodies are built for where they live.

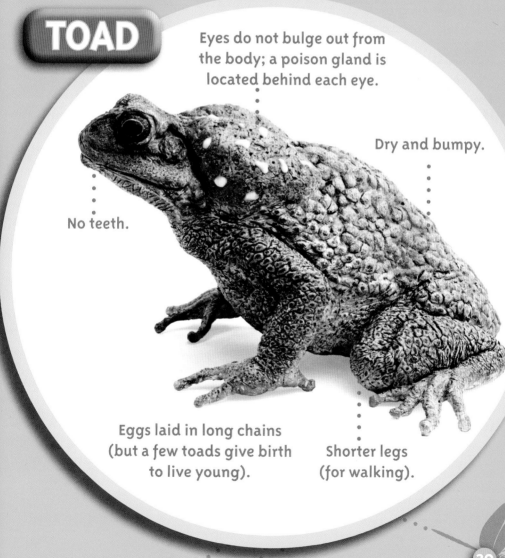

TOAD

Eyes do not bulge out from the body; a poison gland is located behind each eye.

Dry and bumpy.

No teeth.

Eggs laid in long chains (but a few toads give birth to live young).

Shorter legs (for walking).

SUPER FROGS!

TWO-FACED FAKER

A FAKE FACE FOOLS ENEMIES WHEN THIS FROG TURNS AROUND!

TWO HEADS...

...ARE BETTER THAN ONE!!

The HIGH FLYER

WHOOSH!

ANY FROG CAN JUMP, BUT WATCH ME GLIDE!

IT'S A BIRD, IT'S A PLANE!

It's a Gliding Leaf Frog!

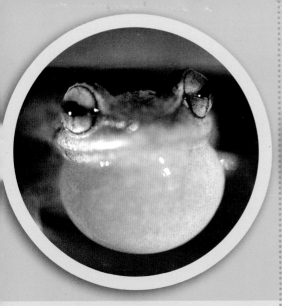

Gills

CROAK
The deep, hoarse noise that a frog makes.

GILLS
The body parts on the sides of a fish or tadpole through which it breathes.

HABITAT
The natural place where a plant or animal lives.

POISON
Something that can kill or hurt living things.